Augustus

A Captivating Guide to the First Emperor of Rome and How He Ruled the Roman Empire

Free Bonus from Captivating History (Available for a Limited time)

Hi History Lovers!

Now you have a chance to join our exclusive history list so you can get your first history ebook for free as well as discounts and a potential to get more history books for free! Simply visit the link below to join.

Captivatinghistory.com/ebook

Also, make sure to follow us on Facebook, Twitter and Youtube by searching for Captivating History.

Contents

INTRODUCTION.. 1

CHAPTER 1 – ROME.. 3

CHAPTER 2 – THE EARLY YEARS 7

CHAPTER 3 – EARLY CAREER 10

CHAPTER 4 – CAESAR'S SON 14

CHAPTER 5 – THE ROAD TO ACTIUM.. 19

CHAPTER 6 – AUGUSTUS 24

CHAPTER 7 – THE BIRTH OF AN EMPIRE.. 28

CHAPTER 8 – IMPERATOR 32

CHAPTER 9 – DEATH AND LEGACY 38

CONCLUSION 43

REFERENCES... 46

Introduction

"Young men, hear an old man to whom old men hearkened when he was young." (Augustus, reported by Suetonius)

The life of Augustus is historically important because his leadership marked out a new era in the story of the Roman world, an era that would see the expansion of the Roman Empire across the Mediterranean and beyond. However, the influence of the Roman Empire extended much farther than its territory and had a profound effect on the development of Western culture.

Moreover, the stories and legends that emanate from the Roman world have become part of the cultural consciousness of the Western world today. Our fascination with the Roman world is boundless; there are thousands of movies, books, plays, and video games that are inspired by ancient Rome. The stories of the lives of great Romans have, in turn, become stories and ideas that have been taken up by everyone from Shakespeare to the Star Wars franchise.

While the language, culture, and societal norms of Roman life were so different from those we know today, to the point that it can be difficult to relate to what life would have been like, many of the issues that affected Rome are strikingly similar to those that affect our modern societies. We may not understand the technicalities of the legislative tactics of the Roman Senate or the religious aspects of their governmental system, but we can certainly relate to the idea of big political personalities struggling for power against a background of propaganda.

It helps to remember that Roman citizens essentially wanted the same things that any citizen wants: security, prosperity, and stability. Augustus offered these things to people who had experienced lawlessness, civil unrest, and political dysfunction. However, the Roman people—and the government—were extremely suspicious of powerful individuals. In fact, the Roman Republic that Augustus was born into was designed to prevent any individual from amassing great power.

What is absolutely fascinating about the story of Augustus is the way that he masterminded his ascent to power by leading people to believe that power was the last thing he wanted, so that as a leader, he was willingly accepted—and often demanded—by the people. At the same time, he also proved indispensable to the Senate, whose job it was to check his power.

Chapter 1 – Rome

The history of Rome can be roughly divided into three distinct time periods: The Roman Kingdom, the Roman Republic, and the Roman Empire. To understand the pivotal role that Augustus played in the shaping of the Roman Empire, first, we have to understand a little of the history of Rome. By looking at the world that Augustus was born into, we can better understand how his life changed the course of history—not just for Rome, but for the wider world.

The Roman Kingdom

From the accepted foundation of Rome in 753 BCE until 509 BCE, Rome was ruled by kings. These kings were of various cultural backgrounds, including Roman, Sabine, and Etruscan origin. This is sometimes called the "legendary period" because many of the stories that we have about this time are a mixture of mythological tales, folklore, and historical accounts of varying degrees of reliability. We do know that the territory of Rome expanded during this time. This would have naturally led to further integration of different cultures, and inevitably, it would have resulted in competition for territory.

Each king was chosen by the Curiate Assembly and had to undergo a ceremony to ensure that the gods agreed with their choice of king. However, once they were appointed, the kings had absolute power. They controlled political issues, military policy, and religious matters. They could make or dissolve laws, appoint or get rid of officials, and were considered to be above the law. Essentially, the king could do as he pleased.

The Roman people, in time, became dissatisfied with the monarchy. There was a strong feeling that the system of government was unjust, and this came to a head with the reign of Lucius Tarquinius Superbus, who would be the last king of Rome. He was a deeply unpopular ruler due to his disrespect for Roman customs and his violent and oppressive tactics in controlling his citizens. The final straw came when his son raped a woman named Lucretia, who was the wife of Lucius Tarquinius Collatinus (who would go on to become one of the first consuls of Rome) and a daughter of an important noble family. As a result, she committed suicide, and her tragic story struck a chord with the people, bringing to the fore all of their grievances about the unfair way the monarchs ruled and the immoral way they led their own lives. As a result, a revolution began that would see the end of the monarchy and the establishment of the Roman Republic.

The Roman Republic

The Roman Republic was founded in 509 BCE and lasted until 27 BCE. It took inspiration from the Greek systems of government, abolishing the old monarchy in favor of a government where, in theory, no one ruler could rise above the rest. This government was to be led by two consuls, each of whom was elected by the population on a yearly basis. The consuls sought advice and guidance from a Senate, which formed to oversee the government. The whole system was designed to ensure that each individual had their power checked and that nobody could make major decisions without the input of others. This meant that the public could be confident that they would not be dominated by a tyrannical ruler.

However, while the Roman Republic was created as a fairer method of ruling the expanding Roman world, it was still not a democracy. Instead, it functioned more like an oligarchy; the role of consul was generally always taken up by a candidate who came from one of the established ruling families. So, while the monarchy had been abolished, there was still a strong sense of aristocracy among the ruling classes. Ordinary citizens still did not have any real power.

The Roman Republic was founded on an unwritten constitution that constantly changed as the government encountered new situations that they had to legislate for. The Senate was a prestigious body of highly respected individuals who would pass decrees and give advice to the ruling magistrates. Closely adhering to the ideals it was founded upon and a system of government that allowed for adaptation, the Roman Republic functioned for more than 480 years.

However, over time, the Roman Republic began to decline. By the 1st century BCE, it was near to collapse. The Senate, which was supposed to ensure that power passed along fairly, was embroiled in fighting among themselves for power. Political violence began to take the place of political discourse, which was a new phenomenon in Rome. Power suddenly shifted to those prepared to use force, and the Senate was increasingly finding itself challenged by the generals that they assigned to expand the territory of Rome.

In 70 BCE, one of these successful generals, Julius Caesar, had been elected to the role of consul. This coincided with a time of serious social unrest and political upheaval; the standard of living was low, and people were dissatisfied with the political status-quo because they could see the vast difference in the lives of those with power and the lives of ordinary citizens. Slavery was rife, and rebellions against slavery became more and more frequent. Military duty had come to be seen as a way to achieve great wealth rather than a way to serve the Roman Republic, and so it was the wealthiest generals who tended to attract the best soldiers and therefore achieve success.

Julius Caesar was a charismatic leader and a military genius, so he was in the perfect position to swoop in and take advantage of the chaos to seize power. In 60 BCE, Julius Caesar and two other leaders, Gnaeus Pompeius Magnus (better known as Pompey) and

Marcus Licinius Crassus, came to an arrangement to share power in what was known as the First Triumvirate. This marked an important point in the history of Rome; Julius Caesar was poised and ready to challenge the very ideals that the Roman Republic was founded on. Julius Caesar would come to be renowned for his short-lived role as dictator over Rome, but his great-nephew, a man who would come to bring about the end of the Roman Republic and usher in the age of the Roman Empire, was only just being born.

Chapter 2 – The Early Years

On September 23rd, 63 BCE, Gaius Octavius was born into an average, relatively comfortable Roman family. He was born in Rome, in a place called Ox Head, but was soon taken to Velletri, a village near Rome where his father's family hailed from. Rome at this time was incredibly overcrowded, and the family felt that Velletri was a better place for the boy to be raised, especially as his father was often away taking care of his duties.

At the time of his birth, Octavius' father, also named Gaius Octavius, was the governor of Macedonia. Octavius' paternal family was *equestrian*, meaning they were the second level of property-based classes (the senatorial class was first); they were a highly respected family that had mostly worked in banking, as well as being magistrates, and they had a history of loyalty to Rome. Octavius' father had been a part of the Senate and was later elected praetor (magistrate) in 61 BCE. His role as the governor of Macedonia at the time of his son's birth was his highest position, and he received much praise for his competent, reliable service and his success in defending Macedonia from attacks by various tribes during his leadership.

Octavius' mother, Atia Balba Caesonia, was the niece of Julius Caesar, making Octavius the great-nephew of Julius Caesar. Caesar was a rising power in Rome, but he was childless at the time. As such, the birth of a great-nephew might have generated some minor attention, but other than this, Octavius' birth would not have been considered important outside of his own family. It is likely that he would have been expected to be a minor politician or perhaps an estate owner managing a farm.

Historical sources tell us that ominous signs around the time of his birth later led many people to believe that his arrival in the world had been foretold and that he was destined to become a great emperor. There had been a prophecy by an oracle that the village of Velletri would be the birthplace of a great leader of the Roman Empire. Respected scholar Publius Nigidius Figulus foretold the greatness of Octavius, while Consul Quintus Lutatius Catulus and philosopher and statesman Marcus Tullius Cicero both claimed to have had visions about the arrival of a great leader. Even Octavius' mother was believed to have had strange dreams while pregnant with him. Whether these omens were genuine or were described with the benefit of hindsight is not known, but they are very interesting to consider.

Suetonius, a Roman historian, shares a number of wonderful (if perhaps not very believable) stories about Octavius as a child. Some of the more dramatic of these include the infant Octavius going missing from his crib. A frantic search party ensued, and eventually, the baby was found at the top of a tall tower, staring at the sky. Other stories, such as the ones in which he is able to command the frogs outside the villa to stop croaking or silently command an eagle to return a piece of stolen bread, all point to the creation of a legend that the Roman people could look to for confirmation of Octavius' predestined authority. Roman culture may have aspired to republican ideals, but it was also heavily religious, and so, people looked for those with political power to be sanctioned by a higher power—the gods.

Octavius the elder returned from Macedonia to a family villa in Nola, Italy, in 59 BCE when Octavius was four years old. The plan was that Octavius the elder would stand as a candidate for consulship the following year. He had gained the necessary support from the Senate to stand for election as consul through his military achievements. This would have been a considerable advancement for Octavius the elder and for his family, and it would have certainly had repercussions on the life of his young son. However, soon after his return to Italy, he died very suddenly. Octavius was left without a father, and the task of educating him fell to his mother, Atia. Just like any Roman schoolboy of his background, Octavius was educated in both Greek and Latin, and his studies would have had a strong focus on becoming a skilled orator.

Atia remarried when Octavius was six years old. Her new husband was Lucius Marcius Philippus, who became consul in 56 BCE. He was politically opposed to Julius Caesar but was not directly in conflict with him, allowing him to have a successful public career. Octavius was sent to the home of his grandmother, Julia Minor—the sister of Julius Caesar. We know very little about these childhood years, except that a number of sources mention that Octavius was a sickly child and often suffered from ill-health.

When Octavius was just twelve years old, Julia Minor died. The young boy gave a powerful *laudatio* (a funeral oration similar to a eulogy) at her funeral. It was at this event that he was suddenly noticed by Julius Caesar, who was immensely impressed by the speech the boy had given for his sister. This marked the beginning of Julius Caesar's interest in Octavius, which was to change the young man's life forever.

Chapter 3 – Early Career

Reaching the age where a boy was considered to be a man was a very important milestone in many ancient cultures, and it still is today; even in modern times, we celebrate when a teenager officially becomes an adult. The tradition in the Roman culture at the time of Octavius placed huge importance on this momentous event when a boy, who would have previously spent his time studying and learning about the society he was going to enter, was suddenly considered to be suitable to hold all kinds of responsibilities despite his lack of practical experience. This day was marked by giving the young man his first toga.

Octavius officially became a man when he turned fifteen years of age on October 18th, 48 BCE. He received his *toga virilis* on this day, which was a white flowing garment that was an important symbol of manhood and permitted him to enjoy the benefits of adult citizenship. While many other young men may have been eased into adult life, Octavius had already attracted the attention of Julius Caesar, and he was very quickly given an important role in society by being elected into the College of Pontiffs in 47 BCE.

The College of Pontiffs was made up of the most senior religious figures in Rome. This undoubtedly caused quite a stir in Roman society at that time; it was unheard of for a man so young and inexperienced to be elected into such a high-ranking position. Octavius had essentially been fast-tracked to a point far beyond that of his superiors. This was more than just a sign of the faith that the establishment had in him, but an important message to the rest of Rome that Octavius enjoyed the favor of Julius Caesar and had a bright future ahead of him.

At this stage of his life, historical sources begin to take more notice of the young man who was making such a stir, which proves useful for historians trying to understand the life of Octavius. We know that he was considered to be good looking and that he attracted a lot of attention when he was presented in public. However, Octavius was very closely guarded by his mother and her family so that he would not be tempted by some of the seedier attractions of Rome. Sources tell us that he was kept away from women to avoid any potentially messy love affairs by taking care of his religious duties before sunrise. His life apparently changed very little, despite his high status; he lived in the same modest chamber, kept the same company, and led a simple life. Whether these accounts of Octavius' model behavior as a cautious and sensible young man were true or a form of propaganda is impossible to say. What we can be sure of is that he was suddenly given a lot of responsibility, as he was in charge of the ancient Olympic games just a year after being elected to the College of Pontiffs. These games had been arranged to celebrate the building of the Temple of Venus Genetrix by Julius Caesar; yet again, Octavius was being introduced as a key figure in the political life of his great-uncle.

At this time, Julius Caesar was at a pivotal point in his career. The First Triumvirate, the coalition that divided power between Caesar, Crassus, and Pompey, was beginning to fracture. Rivalries between the three most powerful men in Rome had escalated into all-out conflict. In 53 BCE, Crassus died, and the battle for power between Julius Caesar and Pompey became even more intense. As the leader of the Senate, Pompey had the power to disband Caesar's armies fighting in Gaul and send Caesar home to Rome. He wasn't allowed to stand for election to consul again, and before long, Caesar felt he had no other option than to mount an attack that meant the outbreak of a civil war. Despite being massively outnumbered, Caesar's forces defeated those of Pompey in 48 BCE. However, there still remained forces loyal to Pompey in Spain, then known as Hispania, who would have to be defeated for Caesar to gain complete power.

Octavius began to express his desire to be more active in the service of Julius Caesar, and while his mother stopped him from joining Caesar's forces to fight in Africa, he was determined to join Caesar in Spain to defeat and scatter the supporters of Pompey. Octavius made plans to join Caesar, but these had to be postponed because he became seriously ill. There are a number of times in Octavius' life when contemporary sources describe him as being unwell, and this is the first time that we see him being unable to carry out his duties or further his aims due to ill health.

However, Octavius was not to be stopped! In fact, what happened next gives us a very clear idea of how determined and capable he was, and it did exactly the same for the people of Rome and those farther afield who heard about his brave escapades. When Octavius finally did leave Rome to join Julius Caesar in Spain, the boat he was sailing in was shipwrecked. Octavius and a small number of other survivors of the accident managed to swim ashore. Here, they found themselves faced with the prospect of an extremely difficult journey across enemy territory in a country they were unfamiliar with. Yet, somehow, they managed to make the trip all the way to Caesar's camp. This was a huge undertaking, and Julius Caesar was extremely impressed with both the practical ability and the commitment to the cause shown by Octavius. As a result, Octavius was permitted to travel with Caesar in his personal carriage and was instructed by him in the ways of governance.

Caesar and Octavius remained in Spain until 45 BCE and then traveled back to Rome. Caesar was now the most important man in Rome, as he had ensured that he held a tight grip on the reins of power by claiming the role of consul and dictator for ten years in 46

BCE. The political situation in Rome was changing, and Caesar had managed to lay claim to more power than any other person since the formation of the Roman Republic. He was planning to extend his power—and the area of Roman control—by going to war with Parthia. To do this, he would need loyal and capable men in the area, poised to take military control.

Octavius was sent to Apollonia in Macedonia—where his father had been governor—to gain a thorough education in military methods as well as academic subjects. He was also given the title of Master of the Horse. This made him the chief lieutenant, second only to Julius Caesar himself. Octavius was a crucial part of Caesar's grand plan for pushing Roman control into the Middle East. However, even more honor was yet to come for the young man, and it was not through a war with Parthia. Octavius was about to gain more power than he could have ever imagined, and by means that Julius Caesar himself could never have foreseen.

Chapter 4 – Caesar's Son

In 44 BCE, Julius Caesar was assassinated. His death has become an enduring legend, and many people know the story of how the senators, including Marcus Junius Brutus and Cassius Longinus, plotted against Caesar and came together in the Theatre of Pompey to stab him to death on the now infamous Ides of March (March 15th). The Senate feared the rapidly growing power and popular appeal of Julius Caesar, and they suspected that he was planning to establish himself at the head of a monarchy. They thought that the only way to protect the Roman Republic they believed in was to rid Rome of Julius Caesar once and for all. A group of these senators cornered Julius Caesar and stabbed him, one by one. In doing so, there was no single killer who could be held accountable for the act.

While Rome was fairly used to the sudden suspicious deaths of leaders, the death of Julius Caesar sent shockwaves across the Roman world, and we can only imagine the impact that the news might have had on young Octavius, who was in training to be an integral part of Julius Caesar's inner circle of powerful men. Octavius' future relied on the support and patronage of Julius Caesar, especially since his own father had died when he was a very young child. His future, which had looked so bright, was now uncertain. In fact, his safety as one of Caesar's most senior lieutenants was at risk.

However, Julius Caesar had one final surprise in store for Rome and for his great-nephew. He had been so impressed by the young man during the time they spent together in Spain that when he had returned to Rome, he had secretly made a new will and left it with the Vestal Virgins for safekeeping. This document named Octavius as the heir and chosen successor of Julius Caesar.

Returning to Rome at this time represented a serious risk to Octavius, and he was warned by advisors, including his stepfather, of the danger in returning to a city that had turned on his patron. Octavius, however, was determined to return when he learned of the contents of Caesar's will. Ignoring the danger, he set out for Rome to claim his inheritance and, in doing so, entered a new phase of his life. When he arrived in Rome, he found that not only was he named as the successor of the leader but that he had also been adopted by Caesar as his legal son.

Octavius took on the name Gaius Julius Caesar and was commonly called Caesar at the time, but historians generally use the name Octavian to avoid confusion with the dictator Julius Caesar and also to mark his new identity as Caesar's adopted heir.

Power Struggle

This news came as an unpleasant shock to Julius Caesar's co-consul, Marcus Antonius, better known as Mark Antony, who had taken over his assets. Mark Antony was fully expecting to be the natural heir of the late leader, who had no legitimate living children that he acknowledged. Antony had gained popular support and had managed to raise public anger against the assassins of Julius Caesar with a powerful speech delivered at Caesar's funeral, forcing Brutus and Cassius out of the city. With this move, Antony was well on his way to securing his own claim to power.

The arrival of Octavian upset Mark Antony's plans, and so began a long-standing power struggle between the two men. Mark Antony allowed Octavian to take on Julius Caesar's responsibilities and pay his bequests to the Roman people, but he would not release any of Caesar's funds, and so, Octavian had to find the money himself. Mark Antony even went as far as to spread rumors that Octavian had only become Caesar's heir through sexual favors. While this was a very common way of questioning the legitimacy of a rival's power in Rome, it was still a damaging suggestion at a time when Octavian was trying to gain the respect of the Roman government and people.

Octavian's determined and resourceful nature won through at this pivotal point in his early career. In need of money, he claimed funds that Caesar had set aside for his planned war with Parthia without permission from the Senate. He also took on the military forces that Caesar had built up for the conflict, reinforcing his own troops with Caesar's loyal military by playing on the fact that he was Caesar's chosen heir. He began to attract many of Caesar's supporters and gathered a formidable army. With money and military behind him, Octavian returned to Rome to face Mark Antony in 44 BCE.

Return to Rome

When Octavian got to Rome, he found that Mark Antony was in an increasingly precarious position, trying to stay in favor with the Roman public and represent the Caesarian Party (supporters of Julius Caesar) while keeping on the right side of the powerful Senate and dealing with the ongoing threat from those who were concerned that he was amassing too much power too quickly and following too closely in the footsteps of Julius Caesar. Having done his best to undermine Octavian's claim to power, Mark Antony decided it was best for him to leave Rome and set out to Cisalpine Gaul, where he had arranged to become governor. However, the province was under the control of one of the men involved in Julius Caesar's assassination, Decimus Junius Brutus Albinus (Decimus Brutus). The handover of power did not happen, and the two men went to battle, enraging the Senate.

This was an opportunity for Octavian to prove himself and gain credit with the Senate, as well as to ensure that Mark Antony was no longer a threat. Octavian was made a member of the Senate and was given the power to command troops so that he could go and join Decimus Brutus to defeat Mark Antony and force him to retreat farther away to Transalpine Gaul. In doing this, Octavian formed an alliance with Marcus Aemilius Lepidus, a powerful candidate who had succeeded Octavius as the high priest in the College of Pontiffs. The Senate reacted to this decisive victory against Mark Antony by rewarding Decimus Brutus and largely ignoring Octavian's part in the proceedings. As a result, Octavian refused to help the Senate any further and instead marched to Rome and demanded that he be the successor of the consuls who had died in battle. This was initially refused, but when faced with Octavian's military force, the Senate had no choice but to elect Octavian to the position of consul, alongside his relative, Quintus Pedius.

The Second Triumvirate

The only way that the battle for power between Octavian and Mark Antony could be resolved, putting an end to the civil wars that had plagued Rome since the death of Caesar, was for an alliance to be formed. Neither man had the power to completely dominate, especially under the careful eye of the Senate. It was arranged for the three men—Octavian, Antony, and Lepidus—to meet at Bologna and find a way forward. On November 27th, 43 BCE, the Second Triumvirate was established. This was a means by which the three men could share power and was designed to last for five years to reestablish control across the Roman territories. While Brutus and Cassius still held power in the east, the three leaders—known now as the Triumvirs—divided the western territory up among themselves. While this afforded them some security from the threat that they posed to one another, it also made them vulnerable to challenges from other powerful characters who either publicly or privately opposed the new regime.

The other issue facing the Triumvirate was finances—money was needed to fund the planned war against Brutus and Cassius, both to avenge the death of Julius Caesar and to secure their provinces.

The solution came to be known as the proscriptions. A (rather long) list was drawn up of men who any of the Triumvirs could consider to be enemies. The conflict may have been political, public, or personal, but there were up to 300 senators and 2,000 knights (a social ranking just below the senators), among many others. Those who were on the list were outlawed. All of their property was confiscated, and those who didn't escape were killed. It was relatively easy to turn the population against the proscribed by simply offering rewards for their capture. This got rid of enemies and potential trouble-makers while filling up the coffers of the Triumvirate so that they could fund their armies.

Octavian found himself in a new, but still difficult, position. The Triumvirate was a delicate balance of power-sharing that relied on trust between men who had so recently been enemies. It was extraordinarily helpful for Octavian when he became—to all intents and purposes—the son of a god.

Chapter 5 – The Road to Actium

In 42 BCE, the Senate decided to deify Julius Caesar, making Octavian *Divi filius*, "Son of the Divine"; he was now officially the son of a god and the heir of the great dictator. Along with this announcement came a lot of prestige and a lot of expectations. However, Octavian appears to have thrived in his new role, and if anything, the new title spurred him on to immerse himself in the challenges that he now faced with confidence. The first of these challenges was to eliminate Brutus and Cassius. This served a number of purposes; firstly, it was an act of revenge against the men who had been responsible for the plot to assassinate Julius Caesar. Furthermore, it got rid of any threat they may have posed while at the same time sending a powerful message to anyone else who might consider wronging him.

Phillipi

Antony and Octavian confronted and defeated Brutus and Cassius at Phillipi in Macedonia in 42 BCE. This was fundamentally a victory for Antony, as he claimed the win and denounced Octavian as a coward who preferred to delegate his military duties to his general Marcus Vipsanius Agrippa rather than stand in battle himself.

Antony was increasingly vocal about his disapproval of Octavian and took the opportunity after Phillipi to align himself with Cleopatra VII of Egypt. Cleopatra was the former lover of Julius Caesar and potentially the mother of his child, Caesarion. It is not known for certain if Caesar ever actually had any living children. Caesarion is the strongest case that Caesar did produce at least one child, but while Caesarion did look a lot like Caesar, Caesar never officially acknowledged him.

Octavian found himself back in Rome with a particularly difficult task at hand. He was responsible for resettling the veteran soldiers who had been promised homes in return for their service. The problem was that there was no land to settle the veterans on. Faced with the prospect of angry soldiers who would easily withdraw their loyalty or, worse, rebel against him, Octavian made a deeply unpopular move. He confiscated land from thousands of citizens, evicted many towns, and cast countless working people into poverty, homelessness, and ultimately death. Unsurprisingly, this lost Octavian a lot of public support.

Meanwhile, Octavian's personal life was also less than happy. He had divorced his wife, Clodia Pulchra, who was Mark Antony's stepdaughter. This had the effect of angering her mother, Fulvia, who allied herself with Mark Antony's brother, Lucius Antonius, and formed an army to fight against Octavian. Lucius had benefitted from the drop-off in public support for Octavian, so this was a critical moment for both men. Fulvia and Lucius Antonius put Octavian under siege at Perusia (modern Perugia, Italy), but he turned the situation around and mercilessly slaughtered everyone who had supported or allied with Lucius. He spared Lucius because he was the brother of Mark Antony, but extensive burning and looting occurred in Perusia, sending a strong message to others not to oppose Octavian.

The Treaty of Brundisium

The Triumvirate still stood, but there was constant competition between the three leaders. Relations had definitely soured between Octavian and Antony. Octavian had been opposed by Antony's wife and brother while Antony had been having a love affair with Cleopatra. The relationship was no mere fling, though; the couple had three children together, and their relationship is still the stuff of legendary romances!

Mark Antony returned from Egypt with the aim of defeating Octavian, but there was no appetite for conflict among the commanders of their forces. Instead, a treaty was set up at Brundisium to reaffirm their alliance and redistribute land; Lepidus was to remain in Africa, Antony would control the East, and Octavian would have power over the West. Mark Antony was given Octavian's sister, Octavia Minor, in marriage as a gesture of unity. For the people of Rome, this was a happy development; they had tired of civil wars and the unrest it brought.

War with Pompeius

Before long, the relationships within the Triumvirate were tested by Sextus Pompeius, the son of Pompey, Julius Caesar's old ally-turned-enemy. Pompeius refused to allow grain to pass through the Mediterranean to Italy, which was under Octavian's control. Octavian had previously managed to stay on good terms with Pompeius by marrying into the family; he married a woman called Scribonia, thought to have been an aunt or sister of Pompey's wife. Scribonia soon fell pregnant and gave birth to a girl, known as Julia the Elder, who would be Octavian's only natural child. However, on the day that Julia was born, Octavian divorced Scribonia, citing incompatibility, so that he could marry Livia Drusilla. This did nothing to help relations between Pompeius and Octavian, and since Octavian did not have the military power to fight him, he was forced to renew the Triumvirate for another five years. Antony sent troops to support Octavian, but Octavian reneged on his promise to send troops to Antony's aid in Parthia. So, once again, the alliance between the two was on shaky ground.

Pompeius was subsequently defeated by an alliance of Octavian and Lepidus, and with promises of money and peace, Octavian managed to poach many of Lepidus' men to join his own forces. Lepidus had little choice but to surrender to Octavian, and while he was expelled from the Triumvirate, he was allowed to keep his office as *pontifex maximus* (the head of the college of priests), although he was essentially exiled to a remote villa.

Octavian saw the tide beginning to turn in his favor, and he negotiated his own safe return to Rome with the Senate so that he could set about gaining popular support from the Roman people. In his half of the empire, he made sure that his citizens had security and the right to property, and he also returned over 30,000 slaves who had supported Pompeius to their former owners. He had learned his lesson about settling veterans outside of Italy, so there was no repeat of the previous turmoil when it came to that issue.

The Battle of Actium

Mark Antony, on the other hand, was not having such a good time. His campaign in Parthia had been a complete failure—no doubt in part due to Octavian's broken promises of support—and he had insulted Octavian and caused an uproar among the Romans by divorcing his sister Octavia Minor in favor of an illegal marriage to a non-Roman, Cleopatra VII. They had already been in a famed romance for many years, and she had borne him three children. Cleopatra could offer Antony the military support he needed, but their relationship was deeply unpopular amongst the Romans and did irreparable damage to his reputation.

Octavian publicly promised to give up the Triumvirate now that peace had been restored, if only Antony would also step down. He knew that Antony would refuse, but it was just a ploy for Antony to receive more bad publicity with the Roman public. Octavian was elected consul and used his position to spread propaganda against

Antony, pointing out that he had been paraded with Cleopatra on golden thrones, that he had given her the title "Queen of Kings," and that all signs pointed to Antony giving Roman power to a foreign queen. These claims were not completely fabricated; after stealing Antony's will from the Vestal Virgins, Octavian was able to prove that he had planned to divide his territory up among his sons and be buried with Cleopatra in Alexandria. It was enough for the Senate to initiate war with Cleopatra.

Octavian was now in a strong position to mount an attack on Mark Antony's forces and cement his claim to power. However, it was not just Mark Antony he had to defeat; it was Cleopatra as well, and her army was formidable. Fortunately for Octavian, his military commanders, including his best general and friend Agrippa, were some of the most experienced and capable. On September 2nd, 31 BCE, their naval forces met at Actium in Greece. Cleopatra's forces suffered heavy losses, and she retreated back to Egypt with many of her ships and those of Antony. Those that remained surrendered. Octavian had successfully broken up her army. It took almost a year before Octavian could achieve a decisive victory against Antony in Alexandria. After the final battle, Antony and Cleopatra committed suicide, and Octavian ensured that Cleopatra's son Caesarion (the possible child of Julius Caesar) and the eldest son of Antony were both killed so that they could not pose a threat to his power. He seized Cleopatra's treasure and used it to pay his armies, ensuring that he could return to a hero's welcome in Rome.

Chapter 6 – Augustus

The Battle of Actium was a major turning point for Octavian and for the Roman Republic. The Roman Republic had not been properly functioning as a republic for a long time due to the civil wars that had sprung up both during the life of Julius Caesar and especially after his assassination. The murder of Julius Caesar was intended to rid Rome of a leader who was amassing personal power; with his death, the Senate could regain control, and the Roman Republic would once again be just that, a republic. However, the ensuing chaos and unrest had meant that power was shared between just a few rivals who divided Roman territory among themselves. This was not how the Roman Republic was supposed to be run, and the Roman citizens were not happy.

Due to a combination of good fortune and great planning, Octavian had rid himself of all of his major competitors in the struggle for Roman power. He was undoubtedly the most powerful individual in the Roman Republic, and yet the Republic was designed to ensure that no one single person would ever have complete control. The Senate was still a powerful institution, and after the rise and fall of Julius Caesar, and the ensuing instability as his would-be successors battled for power, there was pressure from the people to return once again to the ideals of the Roman Republic. Octavian recognized that seizing power by force was not going to be an effective way to become the sole ruler of the Roman world. He needed to somehow win the support of both the people, who were desperate for stability, and the Senate, which was desperate to control the power balance in Rome. What was required was some careful planning and a lot of clever propaganda.

Co-Consuls

After his victory at Actium, Octavian marched triumphantly back into Rome with his most important general, Agrippa, by his side. Octavian and Agrippa were elected to the two consul positions, but Octavian still had to win over the Senate's trust before he could begin to amass any real power. It was a tricky situation for both Octavian and the Senate; he needed their support, and they needed the stability his authority would bring, but they were also naturally suspicious of a powerful young leader with the legacy of Julius Caesar on his shoulders.

Rome at this time was suffering badly as a result of the many civil wars that had taken place. With a government that was focusing on the power struggles and battles going on farther afield, Roman law enforcement had deteriorated, and there was widespread social unrest. Octavian was the only hope for the Roman Republic if it was to return to some kind of stable, productive society again.

The First Settlement

In 27 BCE, Octavian made one of his most important, calculated moves toward gaining widespread popular and political support. In effect, he gave away his territories and armies, transferring ownership back to the Roman Republic, its people, and the Senate. This grand display of relinquishing his own personal power in favor of a return to the traditional values of the Roman Republic was a key tactic in gaining the trust of the Senate and the people. Octavian still enjoyed unrivaled wealth, and his loyalty from those who had fought for him meant that he could easily command a powerful military force if required, so his position was only strengthened by this gesture. It gave the impression that he was not seeking to gain personal power or autocracy but rather that he cherished the ideals of the Roman Republic. He went even further than this, spending his own money to pay for important infrastructures, such as buildings and road networks, to win people over with his public spirit and self-sacrificing nature. It was especially important to Octavian that he give the right impression because he was all too aware that Julius Caesar had been assassinated for his attempts to gain personal power and that he could suffer the same fate if his true aims were suspected.

Octavian Becomes Augustus

Octavian was hailed as the restorer of the Roman Republic. The Senate, in turn, handed him more responsibility, putting him in charge of much of the Roman territory, which encompassed Syria, Gaul, Cyprus, Egypt, and Spain. This was an accepted method of governance in the Roman Republic during times of crisis. The aim was that Octavian would bring stability to these unruly provinces while other areas would be overseen by Senate-appointed governors, or proconsuls, signifying a return to the traditional method of governing in the Roman Republic. Octavian ensured that he had input into the appointment of the proconsuls and considered their authority to be somewhat below his own.

By "reluctantly" agreeing to control this huge swathe of Roman territory for ten years, Octavian could keep up the pretense of wanting the power to stay with the Roman Republic and not with him as an individual. It also gave him control of the majority of Rome's legions, so he had the might of the military on his side. How much of his power was due to the unspoken but very palpable threat of his military can only be speculated by historians. This method of governing the Roman territories came to be known as the First Settlement.

A short time after the First Settlement was established, on January 16th, 27 BCE, Octavian was given the honor of a new title, Augustus. This was the name that he would become best known by, a name with a religious slant that means "illustrious" or "revered." Octavian was now officially known as Octavian Caesar Augustus. It is crucial to keep in mind the fact that many of the members of the Senate who were making these important decisions about honoring Octavian—now referred to as Augustus—actually owed their positions to him. There were many senators who were loyal to Augustus who had helped him to legitimize his power. The granting of this new title was more than simply a new name to go by; it was an outward symbol of his changing role both in the government of Rome and in the minds of its citizens. As well as this new name, Augustus also adopted the title *princeps civitatis*, meaning first among citizens or the first/highest citizen in the Roman Republic.

With this new honor came a host of privileges that would be a visible display of the power and influence that Augustus held. In Roman tradition, outward vestiges of power were important status symbols that instantly told everyone who you were and how important you were. However, Augustus rejected such ideas as wearing crowns or diadems, wielding a scepter, or donning the eminent purple toga that Julius Caesar had made famous. Augustus recognized that if he appeared to embrace the trappings of power too freely, the suspicions of those around him would be raised, and thus, his attempt to maintain the semblance of the Roman Republic would fail.

Chapter 7 – The Birth of an Empire

This is the point when historians consider the Roman era known as the Principate to have begun. The Principate is a term used to describe the early period of the Roman Empire. Historians consider the Roman Empire to have started in 27 BCE, and yet at this stage, Augustus was keen to push the ideals of the Roman Republic still. However, the Principate was essentially a dictatorial regime that was dressed up to look like the Roman Republic. It was not a return to a monarchy (as this would have been absolutely unacceptable to the Roman people), but it was autocracy in disguise.

Augustus patiently gained power by small incremental steps. He maintained a strong military force, including a strong and powerful bodyguard for his own personal protection. He also set about making social and infrastructure improvements and established new trade routes to improve the quality of life for the citizens. All the while, he was gaining power while still selling the idea of himself as the great preserver and protector of the Roman Republic to the Roman people. It was an ingenious way of setting himself up as the emperor without causing controversy or inciting rebellion. By keeping the Senate intact, albeit with fewer members, and consulting them on certain decisions, it looked as though the Roman Republic was functioning as it should when, in reality, Augustus was all-powerful.

The Second Settlement

In 23 BCE, Augustus fell gravely ill. While we aren't sure of the nature of this illness, it was serious enough that he was considered to be dying. At this point, on his deathbed, he assigned his documents to his co-consul, Agrippa, including financial accounts, and signed over all his military authority. He also decided on who should receive his possessions and property. What he did not do, though, was name an heir. This came as a surprise; Augustus had a nephew, Marcus Claudius Marcellus, who Augustus was believed to have favored, and it was expected that Marcellus would be named as the heir. As a very powerful man, Augustus would have been expected to name someone to inherit his authority and position in society, but he realized that this would be a step too far toward imperialism and would provoke hostility among his loyal supporters.

As he recovered from his illness, Augustus recognized the need for a new settlement. The First Settlement had worked well for him, and he was emperor of Rome in all but name. However, there were a number of reasons to consider a Second Settlement, and most of these revolved around the need for Augustus to continue making his rule palatable for those who were averse to the idea of a dictatorial ruler, or anything resembling a monarchy, so that he could become more powerful without raising suspicion or inciting resentment.

First of all, Augustus gave up the consulship. He had been elected as consul each year, but after having held the position for ten years, Augustus recognized that there was a growing feeling that the consulship should be open for other candidates. His act of stepping down made it appear to everyone that Augustus wanted to honor the republican process and allow others the chance to serve. He was still allowed to sit on the consul's platform, and he retained his role as proconsul for territories outside Rome itself, which represented considerable power. In fact, the power that Augustus received in return for giving up the consulship more than made up for his loss of the role; he was granted the power of *tribunicia potestas* (tribunician power) for life, which allowed him to preside over elections, veto any laws he did not want to be passed, suggest his own laws at any time, and essentially undermine laws already passed by exonerating those convicted of a crime. He was not only the leader of the Senate, but he also had the right to convene a Senate meeting at any time and to be the first to speak at any such meeting.

Within Rome itself, Augustus was put in charge of the armed forces, known as sole *imperium* (previously, the task of managing these forces had come down to elected officials). Augustus' existing command in the Roman territories was also extended; he could overrule even the proconsuls who were governing the provinces. All of this meant that the Second Settlement served to consolidate and legitimize his power, not further diminish it. More importantly, his power had been increased through traditional republican means. Remarkably, Augustus had managed to appease those who were concerned about his power while actually gaining more power at the same time.

Public reaction to the new settlement was positive. In fact, the public appears to have invested more trust in Augustus than ever before. In 22 BCE, when threatened with a serious food shortage, they demanded that Augustus be given dictatorial power so that he could solve the problem. As before, Augustus made a show of declining this power but then acquiesced, and the food shortage was solved incredibly quickly. So quickly, in fact, that some suggest that he engineered the entire catastrophe so that he could come to the rescue and gain the trust and admiration of the people. When Augustus did not stand for consul that same year, there was a great outcry. For a number of years, only one consul had been elected so that Augustus would take the other position. The general public did not understand how the Second Settlement would function, and so there were fears that Augustus was being pushed out by the Senate. This made it all the more sensible for the Senate to let the public see that Augustus retained power, again playing directly into Augustus' hands.

The Second Settlement wasn't just a good deal for Augustus; it also allayed the fears of the Senate. There had been worries when Augustus was ill over what would happen if the man who Rome relied upon so heavily should die; with his death, civil war would once again become inevitable. With stability in mind, Agrippa was made proconsul and given powers akin to those of Augustus, if not as far-reaching. Augustus married his daughter Julia the Elder to Agrippa in an arranged marriage designed to secure Agrippa's loyalty and procure grandsons who Augustus could adopt as male heirs. This meant that the Senate and the people had peace of mind, and Augustus had a second-in-command who was loyal to him. Augustus considered the Second Settlement in 23 BCE to be when his reign began, while historians usually use the date when he was given the title Augustus, which was in 27 BCE.

In securing the Second Settlement, Augustus ushered in a period of relative peace and prosperity. The chaotic disruption of the previous years was finally over, and there was an opportunity for the attention of Rome to turn to the building of an empire.

Chapter 8 – Imperator

One of Augustus' most prized titles—and he had many—was that of *Imperator*, meaning "victorious commander." It was under this prestigious title that he rapidly set about completely transforming the Roman Republic into the Roman Empire. Expansion of the empire and improvements at home in Rome was the double-edged sword with which Augustus secured his reign.

Augustus was now free from his role as consul, and so, he was better able to travel and become more involved in implementing change "on the ground." From 22 BCE until around 19 BCE, Augustus traveled across Europe and into Asia, initiating reforms and restructuring as he went. His major achievement during this period was to reach an agreement with the Parthians, who had long been enemies of Rome. This meant peace and stability, but it also proved to be an invaluable boost to Augustus' reputation, as he was able to retrieve legionary standards that had been captured in battle over thirty years prior. Resolving the Parthian conflict without war was the first in a number of deals and arrangements set up by Augustus to protect peace in the empire. The focus of his intentions was stability rather than war.

> May it be my privilege to have the happiness of establishing the commonwealth on a firm and secure basis and thus enjoy the reward which I desire, but only if I may be called the author of the best possible government; and bear with me the hope when I die that the foundations which I have laid for its future government, will stand firm and stable. (Augustus, reported by Suetonius)

This period of travel has another important and intriguing mention in the works of the Roman historian Suetonius when he claims that Augustus had been a part of the Eleusinian Mysteries, a ritual initiation ceremony carried out as an important element of the Greek cult of Demeter and Persephone based in Eleusis. This was an unusual move for a Roman leader, but it gives us some insight into Augustus' personal beliefs and his interest in the religious and the mythological.

On his return, Augustus made a number of moves that hinted at his plans for his successor. He gave responsibility to his stepsons, Tiberius and Drusus, setting them up with military powers. He also adopted his very young grandsons, the sons of Agrippa, and renamed them Gaius Caesar and Lucius Caesar. While these decisions might have previously made others in government, and possibly the public, worry that Augustus was setting himself up as an imperial family and giving authority to his own children, Augustus was too powerful to oppose at this point. Perhaps, more importantly, Augustus was incredibly popular, which basically allowed him to get away with whatever he wanted. This fed into his own self-assured belief in his supreme authority.

Economic Reform

One of the best ways to keep people happy and hold onto power was by adding to the wealth of Rome. To do this, Augustus made a series of sweeping reforms that transformed the economy. He did not do this alone. Instead, he set up the first civil service for the administrative management of the empire. This was an effective solution to managing the complicated economic and administrative duties that were too much for one man, even with personal staff, to control.

Taxes were also reformed, with individual citizens responsible for a poll tax and land tax, but taxes on trade were relaxed to promote trade. Tax collection was centralized to help eliminate corruption. Thanks largely to the peace that prevailed under Augustus, trade thrived. The coinage system was overhauled, and many new coins were produced, new mints opened, and industry was actively encouraged.

A New Rome

One of the things that Augustus is best known for is the extensive construction that he had carried out in Rome. With more money flowing into the city, more investment was made into the city itself. The result of this was a new Rome, as it was entirely transformed during the reign of Augustus. Buildings were renovated, impressive new constructions emerged, and the image of Augustus frequently appeared in the form of artwork and statues. New developments in civil engineering and a revived interest in architecture meant that many of the new buildings were both innovative and attractive. Heavy investment in public buildings brought public baths, temples, and places to congregate, encouraging social events and leisure.

Perhaps even more important to the citizens of Rome was that these infrastructure improvements meant a more reliable, cleaner water supply. The peace outside Rome brought many benefits to its citizens, such as a wider range of fresher food and regular supplies, bringing about a peace of mind and stability to the people of Rome that had not been seen in quite some time.

Art and Culture

Culture also thrived under Augustus, again due in part to the peace. Augustus encouraged writers to pay tribute to Rome (and in turn to him). He championed a revival of literature and the arts, and he dedicated himself as a patron of the major poets. Craftsmanship was also promoted across the empire, and there was a surge in the production of fine items, such as gemstones, glass, silverware, fine pottery, and sculpture.

Cultural beliefs were also reinstated, and there was a rekindling of religious tradition; temples that had fallen into disrepair or been damaged in civil unrest were rebuilt, rituals and ceremonies that had been deserted were reinstated, and people were encouraged to take pride in the traditions and cults that had been neglected.

The Deaths of Lepidus and Agrippa

Augustus became the *pontifex maximus* after the death of the former member of the Triumvirate, Lepidus, in late 13 or early 12 BCE. Soon afterward, in 12 BCE, Agrippa died, proving a major loss to Augustus, who went into mourning for a month and had Agrippa's remains interred in his own mausoleum. He subsequently saw to it that Agrippa's family was looked after and that his children were educated.

After Agrippa's death, Augustus forced Tiberius to divorce his wife and marry Julia. This brought Tiberius even closer to Augustus, helping to build up the dynasty that Augustus was passionate about creating. The marriage may have been calculated to both secure Julia's family and ensure loyalty from Tiberius, but neither Tiberius nor Julia were very happy with the match, and the marriage later ended in separation.

Expansion of the Empire

While life in Rome was better than it had been for a very long time, on the outer limits of the empire, things were very different. Peace reigned for the citizens of the Roman Empire, but Augustus still believed firmly in the divine right of Rome to expand. The aim of the expansion was to protect Rome itself and to ensure that the empire was safe from the threat of invasion from other territories. For the first time, Rome had a standing army.

Augustus relied on his stepsons, Tiberius and Drusus, to push back the boundaries of the empire and expand farther north and east. Between them, they moved the border of the Roman Empire all the way to the Danube River. They also expanded into Germany, although Drusus died in the attempt. Tiberius continued to control the military advancement and was rewarded by Augustus in 6 BCE with the opportunity to share his stepfather's power. However, there was a rivalry between Tiberius and Augustus' two adopted sons (his grandsons, Gaius Caesar and Lucius Caesar), who were now of age. Tiberius left Rome and retired but was recalled to Rome in 4 CE after the deaths of both Gaius Caesar and Lucius Caesar. Augustus adopted Tiberius as his son and granted him powers that essentially made him equal to Augustus himself.

With his successorship secured, the expansion of the Roman Empire continued with further movements into Germany and a larger invasion into Bohemia. At the same time, rebellions had sprung up that had to be quashed before expansion could continue. A well-trained and loyal military force, guided by experienced generals, managed to put down these revolts, but the damage to the overarching plans for expansion was done, and the surge into Bohemia was met with disaster. Three legions of soldiers were destroyed when the Germanic tribes rose up against Publius Quinctilius Varus, the Roman governor. The Roman troops were forced to pull out and instead move to the Rhine to defend the outer border.

Even with this defeat, it can be said that the Roman Empire expanded rapidly and successfully during the reign of Augustus, so much so that it came to be viewed as a golden age of expansion. The peace that reigned within Rome itself had allowed for the standard of living to soar and for arts and culture to flourish, and this period came to be seen as the beginning of a time of peace and prosperity known as the Pax Romana, which lasted for roughly 200 years

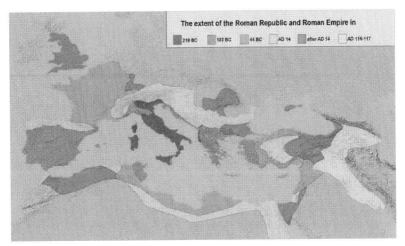

Chapter 9 – Death and Legacy

Augustus' latter years were spent ruling in conjunction with Tiberius. While Tiberius was largely occupied with the expansion and military achievements of the Roman Empire, Augustus oversaw many important social and administrative reforms that had a profound impact on life for the Roman people. The infrastructure that was established at this time in Rome had direct consequences for generations after Augustus' death and was a key reason that the period known as the Pax Romana lasted for so long.

The Death of Augustus

In April of 14 CE, Augustus deposited his will with the Vestal Virgins. Whether he was in ill health or not, sources are not sure. What we do know is that he fell gravely ill sometime later and died on August 19th, 14 CE, in Nola while he was visiting. This was the same place that his father had passed away when he was just four years old, again raising the question of whether Augustus had anticipated his own death.

The last words of Augustus, both those spoken in private and public, have gone down in history and are often quoted for the insight they give us into the mind of the great emperor. To those close to him who were there when he died, he said, "Have I played the part well?

Then applaud me as I exit." His last reported words addressed to the public were, "I found Rome a city of bricks and left it a city of marble." This reference to the drastic changes that he made to Rome perhaps tell us how Augustus wanted to be remembered: not as a powerful emperor, not as a military hero, or not even as a successful leader, but as someone who transformed his beloved Rome and left it a better place than he found it.

The body of Augustus was taken back to Rome, where he was declared a god—the ultimate honor for a Roman leader—and a magnificent funeral was planned. Rome came to a standstill, with businesses closed and people publicly mourning. After his cremation, Augustus' remains were sealed in his mausoleum, known today as the Mausoleo di Augusto. This mausoleum was one of the first buildings to be completed by Augustus and came to be the final resting place for many of his friends, associates, and family members. A large circular building set within gardens and featuring a huge bronze sculpture of Augustus himself, it was a fitting place to inter the emperor, and it remains a popular attraction for those visiting Rome today.

Of course, for a leader such as Augustus to die of natural causes was quite an unusual thing to happen, and rumors abounded at the time and in the years since that he may have been murdered. The most popular conspiracy theory regarding his death is that Livia Drusilla, his wife, poisoned him with figs. Her motive for such an act would have undoubtedly been to secure the role of emperor for her son Tiberius, but this theory is generally considered to have been invented as a form of propaganda by those who favored a different heir following Augustus' death.

Livia did take a very active role in political life after the death of Augustus. She inherited a third of her husband's property, and as she had always been a faithful advisor who was trusted by Augustus to give wise advice, she took the same role when her son Tiberius succeeded him. Augustus adopted Livia into the Julian family in his will, and she was granted the new title Julia Augusta.

Tiberius as Successor

Tiberius was the obvious successor of Augustus; he already had most of the same powers that Augustus himself had, and the two had ruled together for a number of years before Augustus died. However, there was another potential rival for power: Agrippa Postumus, a son of Agrippa, who was given this unusual name because he was born after the death of his father. He had been named as co-heir before Augustus' death but was suddenly exiled in 6 CE for reasons that were never confirmed. Shortly after the death of Augustus, Agrippa Postumus died under suspicious circumstances, rumored to have been murdered by his guards on the orders of Augustus himself or his wife Livia to prevent him from making a claim to power.

Tiberius had already retired from his position and left Rome once before, settling on the island of Rhodes when Augustus seemed set on raising his adopted sons (and grandsons) with the possible aim of molding them into fitting successors. Tiberius was widely considered to be a brilliant general and had many military successes, but there is a pervading sense that he did not really want to rule and had no real love of power. He was considered a serious and somber character, who preferred his own company to the point that he was famously referred to as the "gloomiest of men" by the philosopher and writer Pliny the Elder. He became more reclusive as time went on, and his mother exerted a lot of pressure on him. Eventually, Tiberius left Rome and delegated his duties to his prefects in 26 CE. He lived for another eleven years and died in 37 CE under suspicious circumstances, and he was succeeded by Caligula.

The Roman Empire after Augustus

The Roman Empire that had been born under the guidance of Augustus lasted until 476 CE. The Pax Romana period of stability and prosperity that began with Augustus' rule lasted for around 200 years, and it was during this time that the Roman Empire reached its largest point. In the 2nd and 3rd centuries CE, the Roman Empire began to decline, as it suffered from instability, and it underwent a series of crises that led to the eventual split of the empire into the Greek East and Latin West. The invasion of the Huns, led by Attila, contributed to the decline of the Western Empire, while the Eastern Empire fell to invasion by Ottoman Turks. By 480 CE, the Western Roman Empire was gone; the Eastern Roman Empire lasted until 1453.

Legacy

One of the most widely known legacies left by Augustus is the month named in his honor to celebrate the victories of which he was most proud, especially the Battle of Actium. He chose to rename the month that was previously known as Sextilius after himself, in much the same way that Julius Caesar had renamed July. However, there are many other important legacies that Augustus left behind that are lesser-known but which nevertheless have had a profound impact on the world.

Augustus founded a fire-fighting service in Rome that not only attended fires, limiting damage and saving lives and buildings from the potentially devastating threat of fire, but also served as watchmen. A highly organized group of units patrolled the city at night to keep order. This developed into an early police service, known as urban cohorts, which protected the city and its people from civil disorder, riots, and outbreaks of violence.

The phrase "All roads lead to Rome" is a testament to the sheer number of roads built under the command of Augustus. He recognized that better roads meant better trade, easier mobilization for armies, and an easier life for citizens who now found themselves able to travel to do business. It wasn't just roads that appeared under his rule but bridges, aqueducts, and trade routes. This opened up the Roman territory in a way that had never been seen before, and this was a policy that continued long after Augustus' reign. The fact that many modern roads in Europe are Roman roads that have been updated over the many years is an amazing testament to the infrastructure built up by Augustus and his successors.

Roads that people could travel along for trade purposes meant trade flourished, and this required currency. Augustus saw the development of a uniform currency system, and this system was adopted far beyond the Roman Empire. In fact, many of the innovations of the Roman Empire were developed farther afield. The postal service is an excellent example of this. Augustus set up a series of relay points so that messages could quickly and easily be sent, which later became a postal system that inspired similar systems elsewhere.

Augustus left a lasting legacy, and in fact, it could be argued that few other leaders have had a more profound impact on the world. Within the Roman Empire, we can see the building blocks of modern societies, as well as its impact on government and infrastructure, not to mention law, philosophy, and religion. The impact of Roman architecture can be seen in the neoclassical tradition that is used in practically every city in the Western world. The literature that came out of Rome is still read, performed, translated, and studied by scholars all over the world; think of Horace, Virgil, and Ovid, to name but a few. Our English language would not be what it is today without the Latin of Rome that underpins it. The spread of Christianity can also be largely attributed to its adoption by Rome. The true extent of the effect that the life of Augustus has had on the world in the past 2,000 years is simply beyond measure.

Conclusion

Augustus forged a path to become the first emperor of one of the most powerful and influential empires the world has ever seen. His method of disguising his empire as a republic and hiding his hunger for power behind a façade of traditional values meant that he was able to effectively create a gradual transformation into the kind of rule that he desired. With patience and cunning, he went on to become one of the most famous leaders ever to have lived.

His determination to succeed, despite the dangers, despite the setbacks, and often despite the need for violence and deceit, makes him one of the most fascinating figures in history. While the historical sources tell us little of his character, we are left to deduce what Augustus the man may have been like by studying his deeds. What we are faced with is a contradictory picture.

On the one hand, Augustus was a brutal leader, a general who was ruthless in his quest to conquer and expand the Roman Empire. On the other hand, he established a lasting peace in Rome and made sweeping reforms and changes that undoubtedly made life better for the people of Rome. While history continues to judge the deeds of Augustus, the one thing that continues to evolve is the legacy left by the man and his empire.

Read more Captivating History Books about Ancient History

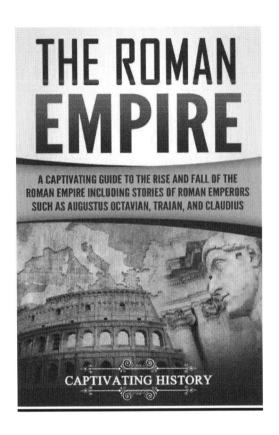

References

(2019). Retrieved 5 November 2019, from

https://www.history.com/topics/ancient-rome/ancient-rome

ancient Rome | Facts, Maps, & History. (2019). Retrieved 5 November 2019, from https://www.britannica.com/place/ancient-Rome

Blackstone, W., Priestley, J., Furneaux, P., Foster, M., & Mansfield, W. (1967). *Commentaries on the laws of England, in four books*. Buntingford [England]: Layston Press for Oceana Publications, New York and Wildy & Sons, London.

McGill, S. *Augustus*.

Mellor, R. (2006). *Augustus and the creation of the Roman empire*. Boston:

Bedford/St. Martin's.

Payne, R. (2009). *Ancient Rome*. La Vergne: J. Boylston & Company,

Publishers.

Roberts, T. (2000). *Ancient Rome*. New York, NY: Metro Books.

Rome Tourism and Travel Guide - Visitors Travel Guide. (2019).

Retrieved 5 November 2019, from https://www.rome.net

Rome.info > Rome tourist information. (2019). Retrieved 5 November 2019, from https://www.rome.info

Shotter, D. (2005). *The Fall Of The Roman Republic*. Hoboken: Taylor &

Francis Ltd.

Simpson, J., Roberts, P., & Bachem, P. (2005). *Ancient Rome*. New York:

Barnes & Noble Books.

Suetonius Tranquillus, G., & Rolfe, J. (2001). *Suetonius*. Cambridge

(Mass.): Harvard University Press.

Tanner, J. (2000). Portraits, Power, and Patronage in the Late Roman

Republic. *Journal Of Roman Studies*, *90*, 18-50. doi:

10.1017/s0075435800031312

Williams, J. (1999) *Augustus*.

Printed in Great Britain
by Amazon

44856256R00035